Surety

Surety

Anna Zumbahlen

Surety

ISBN: 978-1-955969-54-3
Library of Congress Control Number: 2025945466

Poems from this manuscript appeared, sometimes in other forms or with different titles, in *Ambient Receiver*, *UCity Review*, *december*, *Dusie*, *The Maine Review*, and *The Iowa Review*.

Executive Director: Cati Porter
Book layout & design: Hadley Hendrix
Cover art: a derivative work from a photograph by Alex Henderson
Title lettering: Tony Legato

Printed and bound in the United States
Distributed by Ingram

Published by Inlandia Institute
Riverside, California
www.InlandiaInstitute.org
First Edition

For Noah

Seeking Air

Still ideals approach through rendering rains and profiles.
                    If not called *acreage*, at least projected
onto vanished furrows and equivalents of necessity.
                          Sneezing, willful pressure.
                    An atmospheric pressing.
                          Pressurized regression,
tins of fish, boxes of apples. Then simmer
          assumes a previous shape, gestures with weather,
                    loops along, a month with rounded corners.
              A quiet, problemed swell, though reasonably
well-behaved, considering. Beneath the condensation
      that edges in, the house with its soft tasks,
                    a spreading. A day as usual,
                                with difficult edges and interludes.

August

Everyone says the summer will come back,
but it feels like fall to me—

one tree downtown already reddening.
Is afternoon sweet because of the popcorn factory

or because the cornfields have expired and it is August,
acorns on the roof, all night.

Sudden lakes, the ladybugs
and the light, and fields in various states

of harvest. I got involved in things.
Acts of reconstitution

in series and in parallel, when it comes
to shade or shadow, and on farming:

If you don't grow up with it I don't know how
you could teach it—

They seeded this field with an airplane,
and I'm surprised at how well it turned out—

or that it was in bad grammar,
people who'd ended up here by accident.

Overalls told me that if I tune to AM on dark,
clear nights, it's possible to pick up stations

from Colorado. He told me I have an advantage
over others because I'm polite to strangers.

When, again?

In April.
Oh, yeah. Yeah.

I think all the time of your call when I was driving
back to town from the canyon.

The normalcy, you said, an accusation,
and I worry that one day is becoming

my entire summer. Crickets and cicadas
and crashing acorns—it is summer but very nearly

autumn and nothing is silent. The false threat
of the storm that is wildfire smoke from Canada

in front of the sun, acorns on the roof louder than
I'd known to expect. Absolute stillness, impossibility,

the dusk, two then three fawns, and us inside
our heads. A small release and I am thinking of you,

how you invented the life inside your apartment
before you. My wrists are angles incidental to sleep.

Hair too long in the left eye and no favors in the wind.
Early Sunday, no lit storefronts,

no summer children on bicycles.
A hesitation in the weather.

They said sit wherever you want
and watched—your whole torso in backwards,

the sun on his cheekbones, breaching
an unretractable. Altogether clean.

You did not associate this day with its hard
parameters but could see why one would.

Sterile and warm hotel. An argument on the local news.
You drifted, the small relief of a voice
through the phone.

I could say easily that I knew you.
Memory signaled and you
tugged on its edges.

The yellow around and then bare.

Sudden September and filing,
a series of interviews. *Her tic is eye-rubbing,*

when, as if in explanation, you are told
a violence. This could be called an overstepping.

I could name it a gruesome intimacy. Her blonde hair
streaked teal and red and you focus on this

while she lists her very best friends, thumbs her left eye
when you ask her her greatest fear.

The town's minor yawns.

Someone once told you that you are laden with snow.
Having carried this and tended to it and written it into fictions

you have failed to extract the source of its truth.
This is true, that we feed each other from the same tree.

Morning fog too low, unnaturally low and uncertain
in gray light. By midday burned

almost completely off, a supple golden
beam angling on the road.

She rubbed a honeycrisp against her jeans
and held it out, remembering to you

the farmers who brought a prize watermelon
to reciprocate the kindness of her orchard.

Tall grass strewn with apples, apple-rot,
inured to falling fruit, the cloying autumn.

I would like to make a claim about grace,
claim the persistence of a reasonable pattern.

But there's such a thing as incorrect growth,
incidental dispersal.

Aloneness descended all at once. The real town
sketched in the margins of half-said things, or maybe
it's not vital to perceive a whole.

Enough to appreciate a bright afternoon,
reduce the day to manageable parts.

Driving west across the state from Iowa City.
A German pastry shop, autumn dust, golden
cornfields, some razed
and some left standing, drying out.
The usual thrift store: stoneware and histories,
lupines hand-painted on a stemmed glass.
Yellow land, overwhelmingly yellow,
sky and the day moving across it.

Back at home, in the slow cooker:
strips of beef, tomatoes, red peppers, olives.
Later, or another afternoon: apples spiced
with cloves, cinnamon, brown sugar.

I drove due north out of town to the orchard there
and bought regents by the bag, tucked dollars
into a wooden drawer, apples priced
by variety and trusted to the honor system,
and acorns in the grass and on the roof,
turmeric milk and cinnamon, sensory
impressions gesture toward the tonal whole.

And how visible, visibly, do I need this grace
when it has not yet landed anywhere.

What's left: the body, breathing.
A figure taken on the whole

or beneath a moving season,
and I may not know what aggravates the splinter of grief

but the storm hovering like some dark bruise,
but a reflection of leaves turning, a river
toxic with farmland runoff,

or mollusk shells on the bank,
a forest contained by acreages with only deer passing through.

Lend it some dimension, not precisely cinematic,
but with a suggestion of movement,
and the slippage of arriving back

to the same room, a lighted oak anchoring every season—

Summer Sequence

Via the Des Moines River,

the Raccoon is part of the watershed

of the Mississippi River.

The river runs through an intensely cultivated

area of croplands and livestock farming, receiving

tile drainage from slow-draining

rich natural bottomland.

(If you didn't grow up with it, I don't know how

you could teach it)

Where slow-draining rich natural

bottomlands have been tiled to drain them

for agricultural cultivation,

spring thaws and rainy spells

wash nitrate from fertilizer into the river.

On November 20, 2014 nitrates spiked

at 13.7 parts per million (ppm), making the water

unsafe for pregnant women and infants. At the time, these

were the highest readings in the nation.

Tile drainage removes excess water from the soil

below its surface, a sort of *plumbing*.

Iowa's counties (99) are on a grid, more or less.

Polk County (Des Moines)

against Sac, Calhoun, Buena Vista

in the water quality dispute. Nitrates in the water.

Did we worry about the water underground.

Such a verdant spring and summer, I repeated this

commentary, I said *so green* over and over.

Nemaha

It was a cool expanding, a seam exposed.

And then recursion occurs,

gentle reflex. I hear it identify itself moving

up and splitting the image into its various eras.

Oak tree applied to the absence of a viable aphorism.

Lighted by summer, and then those acorns falling.

Tuning variously up, and then down. Snow and snow.

Such an image does not depict an ideal, although it has

been degraded to do so. The uncertain city placed squarely,

again, on the acreage. Regaining composure

through intentional distancing, a moment of grounded

ordinariness, the sun moving behind that barn.

Of course, *taking up residence* is not the same as *prospering*.

Opacity is not the same as *privacy*. Plaintive

without sentimentality. A seam running through.

Laying It Out

Your storm is seeping south
at a rate of twenty-seven miles
per hour both toward me
and away. It appears at once,
a wash, though already
retreating.
               There is no one else
for whom this moment,
this raincloud, is *it*, or *now*,
and presently this *now* no longer
belongs even to me, but my
mind is a slope and the sunset
is somewhere west, moving
                         decidedly away.

July

It took some searching to know I was made
        to stand humid summer, shrill and grown.
                That I sound defended.
That my acts are deliberate and burning
        and neat. Water keeps a memory of the shape
                it's taken and fights to return.

This was a personal weather.
        Rain at the expense of rain.
                The tone shifts—
a thing that happens and can be ordered,
        though not prevented, this problem
                of discerning feeling from experience.

Indicators

I reduced you to your ordinary
physiology and understood
that I would have to learn
anatomy all over again. You
are warm and then
dissolve into a series
of colors and tones.

When I lose interest
in a given moment, I try
to examine it in both of two
ways. So to replay this movement.
So to break my presence down into
more palatable particles
and not have to swallow so hard.

Increased and Spread

First of all, consider the space,
the brick wedged in the door,
the creak of the stairs. Your neighbor moved away,
finally, and left you a book, which you accepted
because its first poem moved you.
Its second did not, so you tossed it aside.
I shivered in your bedroom as though the weather
were your doing.
Yield to your environment,
stretch in a thin rectangle of sun.
Movement for which language has no key,
for which words will be a mute cipher.
Green evening, churchbell lullaby.
The hostas have more than tripled in size.
As usual, I've been asking the wrong questions.
I've lived here all these months and still
I don't know why the deer don't come near
my garden.
Now, consider the river, and consider the fact
that when you found me
I was fully convinced that west was north and that
the river was flowing the other way entirely,
though this is a problem of attention, of course.
I am performing a self-reading.
That you have caught me off-guard is not your fault.
I've been told that after a significant change
it takes your dream-life months to catch
up with your waking world.
That I should expect to dream old normals
until my new normal begins to wear at last.

Drainage Network

This is what I know more than
I know anything else:
solitude is entirely sensory.
I'll admit that I laugh easily
now, though I will not hold you

responsible. This tangible warping
of weather touched down
near an old home while
my local wind pushed water
from air, slow and under

cloud cover. I would like to only
be exactly here, but extreme
presence bears the
            cost of language.
I've decided to trust your ability
to manage ambiguity. You wouldn't

know it, there's no indication, and
eloquence is a relative of quiet.
I would like to save the image
of the wet space beneath my window,
at once a dense and sprawling thing.

Imposing a narrative is key to understanding
the story, this tilting toward the literal.
I cannot cope with this literalness. I will
diminish it until I can carry it,
until it sits silently
                on the page and has no reality.
                I am grateful and so thirsty
                that I almost cannot stand.

Finely

She wrote to me about
the hummingbird
outside her window,
locked in quiet combat
with the summer.
She has such a minor body,
she wrote.
          I don't often see birds
here, though I can hear them.
I ought to feel bereft.
Something so
simple as the spring might
have been handled with
          a little more grace.

Entrenched

This morning I walked farther than usual
and the town felt quieter, greener, full up
with wet sweetgrass, the heady smell of beets,
one bright-winged bird. The jade house
on the corner of 9th has been for sale
for years. It caught fire once, and no
one wants to live there now.

Lately I've sought stories about
the countryside. Often these recount
horrific deaths by bandsaw or by combine,
slow accidental deaths by loss
of limb, and one about a slow
drowning in a grain silo.

                    I am too morbid,
this is over-indulgence.

What I mean to say is this:
we're all working toward repair.
These afternoons are fodder for
something more soft.

Wet Soils

The entire town shows hail damage.
We were built for roof-life,

but this undoing is still
so sincere and in goodwill.

I have the wrong vocabulary
for describing the color of this day

but I can tell you
that I dreamed of so many bees

and took this to be a good omen.
The sod has come loose,

the pesticide truck has already
been by twice this week,

rain too heavy for anything to stick.
It seems autonomy is an extravagant expectation.

Downstairs, a girl stamps her foot
and declares that her cider is not cider

and so she does not want it.
I understand this, for I also

have never been good about keeping
things nice or clean.

Finely

The river is the answer to give me time.
        It remembers the innumerable
authentically but ruthlessly—these
        adverbs have a handle on the present.
I, however, am committed to the dream
        of a new language within which
I would be exempt from meaning
        and intent. This speaks to the fragility
of particular examples. You are a very good example,
        except that no one knows what of.
You're only syllables, barring that
        this doesn't disappear you.

Blooms

You have presented an exercise in patience—
        a new vitality or otherwise nothing
more than vibrant lights behind my eyelids.
        In this context, I think I most mean misinformation.

                The basil plant in the windowsill
has turned all of its leaves southward,
        but I fall asleep with the curtains drawn.

Before I met you, time did not present itself
        as an unbounded succession of ends,
but growth is not linear beneath such a variety of cementings.
        I will acknowledge the guilt implied by the balance
between angry and young if you agree to,
        in this moment, listen.

Verdant

I had planned to control myself this year
but have instead abandoned myself to impulse

the sun cutting a high silhouette

at the reedy scent of cut grass and
fields at various stages of growth

I stop watching and pale
at these vowels

and when I catch my reflection off-guard

I am so

sorry at her bewilderment

Movement

Just beyond countyline I found chicory,
stopped to pull at stems, held this neat
blue tangle until Omaha where all but

one bloom had closed. We go forward
or we go back. Such processes reasonably
well understood, though not

        sufficient enough impetus
        for change. I've missed you,

        imperceptible as some progress is,
        this slow wasting.

Wildfire smoke from Canada yawned
beneath the sun for days and I knew
that if I saw it then you, hundreds

of miles north, had too. Only a string
of coincidences would validate
such flux. We could not palate

        this shortsightedness,
        but wished to.

April

Out of Season

Collaging might sound deeply weird—
remembering, from December, furrows thick with
insects, from December frozen with crossings.
The Raccoon River cleaves the town, and this river's
behavior as it approaches Main Street might appear
fitful, veering through acreages and so on,
diminishingly on, toward Des Moines
where a confusion like a pollutant descends on it,
a real chemical, beneath soils and furrows, clay tiles
and the seepage of the salted river, while cars creep
north, Minneapolis, or south, Kansas City,
late afternoon crossing the expanse of highway,
corn fields and bean fields cropping up beneath it.
Slow blink of lightning bugs, verdant reserves of parks
with their rusting implements, the solitude

of the cemetery and the bridge over the Raccoon
enclosed by chain link. The place persists in existing,
though temporally remote, geographically estranged.
In my notebook, I wrote: *Iowa—intense*
weather systems. A muralist from Florida, some other
visitor, had painted skies on Main Street's empty
brick buildings: a static fog, out-of-climate evergreen,
a prism breaking white, and a dove. Meanwhile
I encountered with estranging wonder the prairie
roses (a ditch weed, like thistles) and the sale of
perennials at Thistle Down Nursery, flowering
trees to plant out at the farm, a vining pea
plant on the trellis, subterranean beets and carrots.
And then we'd grill out, frozen meat, sweet corn,
shake tabasco into light beer.
A tendency to inhabit an earlier version of myself,
and five interceding years, resisting the urge

to name it—quotidian and temperate,

and homesick for anger.

Damp morning, early sun on August-high cornfields.

Daisies pressed in waxed brown paper.

All along here, coercions.

Where and how to place blame: soybean seed sales,

hog farms. How to define the parameters

of productive crossings, waterways

and agricultural waste, algae blooming in

Black Hawk Lake. I tend to be internal,

to romanticize, and, even if a sensory

experience is substitutable, to have an adjacent

bodily experience, though writing about sounds

not immediately present can result in counterfeit

descriptions. Self-containment as forming a stable self,

another kind of agenda. *Enhancing their local assets*

while preserving qualities that make them unique.

Is it always the case that one

form of extraction leads to multiple forms

of extraction, that I can find whatever I need

inside the slippage of language.

It was early April and the fields were tilled.

No more significant snows, but it rained

that first night, a heavy rain, and wind on the lake.

The Racoon River widens as it travels south.

A cultivated green, or a natural one, too.

Des Moines stuck with its water. I imagine it salty,

wrong for thirst. Not even the vegetables

(zucchinis, beets, beans, tomatoes, little peppers)

in the garden out at the farm grow organically.

Insurance against hail damage. Meat always a little

overcooked. No linear path through the county,

nor a circular one. A myopic view of the place:

the landscape radiated out of the experience

of the place. I reread the novel to try to return to some
felt knowledge. The towns, their cafes, the gossip,
the grain elevator. A cold night, but no snow.
Lightless, without even a snow glow.
That reducing an experience to anecdotes
(narrativizing for someone absent) complicates
sensory recall. And reverence for a texture:
pancake breakfast, shoreline clean-up. *Phosphorous
is a big contributor to algae growth in Black Hawk Lake.
Remember to use only phosphorous-free lawn fertilizers!*
Lake View Hometown Pride: removing volunteer
trees in designated areas; will continue to seek outside
funding; loan forgiveness for the city; *with your help,
we'll make it through snow removal season.*
I had a yellow wooden dresser that leaned. Prairie
roses and thistles (ditch weeds, flowers).
I only legibly wrote the summer: summer odors,

summer colors, a heaviness of storms, or not storms:

humidity and cloud cover like a bruise.

Windowsill herbs, thyme planted in an old blue

coffeepot with a hole in its base. *To advocate and*

promote the general welfare of Black Hawk Lake

and the surrounding environments.

The gage located in Sac County, IA on the right bank 5 ft

downstream of the bridge on County Highway, 4.6 miles

south of Sac City, 0.3 miles upstream from drainage

ditch 73, 2.1 miles upstream from Indian creek and

367.6 miles above the mouth of the Des Moines River

at this gage, the Raccoon River's latest data shows

7.37ft, flow 125 CFS

Provisional data subject to revision

so that we might keep them in mind, or keep in mind

the scope of a body's movement in time, a wavering blue,

or displacement of lack into lack,

or want into want. This refinement brings me

neither closer nor pushes me further

outside, early, casting shadow,

golden hour, oak trees. *Lake View has a great*

reputation for strong volunteerism.

Bring your gloves and brush loppers,

maybe even a chainsaw. The river a more significant problem

because it's not so contained, a city can't oversee it.

What pancake breakfast would raise enough

funds for the water treatment facility in Des Moines?

A mostly free-flowing river surrounded by rural areas

in a wooded valley, *it is known as a place of solitude*

and good fishing. Channel catfish, bullhead,

smallmouth bass, flathead catfish, walleye,

on down to Polk County.

Hagge County Park: the oak's heavy leafing

limned in light

given, pressed, shaken, and running over

loose, and spectral

I appreciate that. I'd like to make use of that.

Or that we wait for ice to melt, and it's water that we

consume. Without a static boundary between present

and past tense, transpiring action and past action.

I befriend and integrate the feeling.

Fog today, and the hostas.

Ice floes, bright sediment.

To preserve and protect the Black Hawk Lake

and its watershed. What are the implications of *here*

and its weather

but the shock of small wonders.

A fast walk near the lake—fireflies.

On the porch we shared the beer you brought,

which loosened things.

Dusk invades us, impulses of syntax. *Land is fixed*

albeit subject to all sorts of vicissitudes.

The scale of farmland: navigable by county roads paved

(or graveled) for green tractors *moving at speed.*

When description is already a kind of commentary—

noticing itself is a kind of commentary—

is discernment more extraction, or is it a translation,

reading at a remove. The sounds are incontrovertibly

specific: the hailstones, the acorns,

the insects in the ditch. An exercise in patience

that might yield misinformation.

Memory's erasure and its reconfiguration.

A space held out for someone—

for you—

a presence not manifesting.

Turning the plow, break a line.

"Acre" became a measurement of work applied to earth,

then a measurement of earth surface, part of an intricate,

sensible system of measurement.

intricate, sensible

measurement and description

Another April persisting beneath this one,

another city with its own weather: starker, drier.

In it, a violation, a pink bruise on my neck,

rupture without recovery, the safety

of the room split wide open. Safety split.

Soft cotton of the bed turned over. In the mirror

I could not meet my own eye. Deep ache

between the legs, a refusal. Around

the ways to articulate this kind of hurt. Or to

stay grounded in the real world with its real things:

how many sides does a stop sign have. Count them.

*We must be good stewards of the lake!
We can each make responsible choices that protect
and enhance our lake.*

*The City is a partner on two large projects to be undertaken
this year: (1) a larger fish barrier and pump
station on the inlet; and (2) green infrastructure to
handle the water run-off from the new residential
development on the east of the lake called "The Landing
on East Shore."*

All enjoying the clean lake water.

I wrote the same tree over and over. Lighted
by dawn or dusk, not midday. Always late

summer, early autumn. Always spring.
The winter passed largely unrecorded.

Neighbor's cat swiped at my ankles
when I came to feed her. Brought in the mail.

My air conditioner edging out of the window,
but I was away in Minneapolis. The humid

Saturday, music on a stage, a miscommunication,
a hunger. Heavy wet edging in.

Tile drainage removes excess water from the soil
below its surface, a sort of plumbing.

What gestural memory, or filling in what gaps
in knowledge or attention.

Dismissals, degradation, a question of what gets lost,
or the question beneath my question concerns
how intention and reception won't always correspond,
no easy correspondence between intention and reception
so the vibrations inside the moment mix with others
(other moments, and other vibrations).
I've forgotten what it was I said I'd rather be doing,
laying gravel, pulling sharp grasses, young forsythia,
all apple trees, fruit, fruited as adjective,
slow landslide, slipping topsoil, toward the truth beneath
what I'd said and a doubt installs itself,
unsettles something of the blue
both floral and verbal, a reverence for another texture.
It was okay to hear you real-time.
It was also okay to remember, later, displace emphasis
a little, or a desired emphasis.
Soon it was dusk (fireflies)

and I guess what I'm saying is when you returned, you asked

whether I had forgotten at least some of the detail,

but something persists, how to be encyclopedic without

losing a sense of real presence—

April

I have been immersed in the leafing of trees.

June: riverside brass, trombones.

Such a reversal might be called a judgment.

Last night I dreamed of the mountain,

and there was no trace of you.

Real Weather

Disclosure Becomes Vowels

What I withhold is a preemptive sort of expression, or
response to an expression of weather turning over, subjected

to an intervention of rooms and other people. Overabundance,
florid overwhelm, and then a storm. A darker blue giving over

to reflective yellow. But this storm, this blue, it belongs in
some other year, that year with its continuing resound.

An imagined storm with imagined recursions. Present reality:
a constancy that descends into weather and rebounds

always into a starker blue, angle of hard light. Cultivated
green and its sunfading. I am answering now to a series

of floors and corners, hidden to myself or to you. At a point,
of course I recognize what shape exposure could take,

what I've foreclosed or invited in allowing
witness. In allowing your witness.

Our skin—our soft yes with a bent toward uncertainty.
It may be that refusal is a requirement of closeness, or is it

a repercussion of our indeterminate together.
And the pleasure held there.

A hesitancy that we might not hear reproduced

or a corrective tendency

Was she concerned that the act of

speaking might fix something

make it truer or at least held

or is that my concern

the catching

Hesitancy in the weather

On Tuesday August 13 the City experienced high Nitrate levels in the drinking water. Water tested over the permissible level of 10 mg/l at the Water Plant, but never tested over the limit in the system. In an abundance of caution, a notice was given to the public that infants under the age of six months should not drink the water as Nitrates can pose health problems in young infants. This issue has since been resolved and water is again safe to drink for all.

T*he chain link fence was a false memory*, you said.
I have a distinct memory of this sentence, though
probably you didn't retain it, and that loss is something like
a body recording the passage of time but memory
failing to mark a moment. Or does its quality of being
shared change something in the stakes.

Riverside trailer, Red Cross. Failure and blue bruise.
Lost consciousness. Vulnerable. Regained it like
an opening. Roll this, squeeze this.

Warm. Drift and return into panic.
An absence in your throat. You watch.

Did you know there
are clams in the
river and the
raccoons feed on
them? It's true, but
the river is
too high in nitrates
and phosphates, too
low in oxygen.
Farmland runoff.

Lightning bugs in
the ditches, and
thistle.
Green evening,
looks like rain.

A sandstone gorge. A tributary.
State park.

They'd called it a canyon.
Not a strenuous walk.

On the trail, I met a man practicing
his breath, met his dog, and I have

to say I don't appreciate strangers
asking me where I'm going, but
this happens often in Iowa.

N*o Open Burning of leaves and landscape waste this fall.*

Fog today, and the hostas begin. Clean
of decay. As if washed in tea.

And anyway, I'm not sure I could have said
these things to you without a particular hardness.

Grease shimmer
on stew surface, or

what constitutes the physical
terrain of a memory.

This private act of hope.

Warm light in the bar, velvet.
Bitter beer, Dubuque.

Harsh mid-morning
light, flat glare. Toward midday

filtered through leaves, and cooler.
There was that lake

off Highway 20, a small lake,
a park, not drivable

all the way around. A man with two
small children picnicking.

Some rain, and then the drive home.

Lately, raspberry bushes in Peoria

Low evening in Dubuque

Or an act of intuition

Or a long experience of hope

A tarp to block the wind

A tarp over loose dirt

This slow wasting

Variable
Weather

Okoboji, an air-conditioned conference room,
to discuss mental illness as quantifiable,
a public health issue. The intention is a reclamation
of agency, place trauma on a point scale.
Is quantification a gesture toward narrative.

I am interested also in the resonance of the day,
the significance it imparts elsewhere.

I drove to Iowa on an April Tuesday and it stormed
through that first night. Words cheat silence to build
sentences. It was all very arbitrary.

If words don't move the way water does,
what is there to be faithful to?
Held in place but unable
to describe. The accident of speech.
Whether I become necessarily enmeshed in.

Racoon River to the left. Early April,
a movement out of winter. I meant
to walk as far as I could, to see where the path
might dead-end into an acreage or into the bridge road
or into a cornfield. I trusted the path and did not

bring my phone, did not bring keys, hands empty,
and when I heard the ATVs, I turned and ran and did not
stop until my kitchen. Deep well of shame.
The grooves the memory plays on.
How is this distrust serving me.

Language is very good, though, for providing form.
There could be fissures, interference
with time, of space, but there is also a sort of fixity,
simultaneous nearness and farness. I loved Iowa's

seasons, and so on the page
my fear of aloneness on the path split
into two: one fear, the worse fear, less centered
on the remoteness of the early spring woods

than on other people. My personal narrative,
or my own mythologizing. I made you into
an archetype and addressed myself to that.
Over and over, still do. I would like to remain

open to possibility, but the truth is I knew,
even before, what conclusion I would draw.
Melancholy is fixed. Mourning is a working-through.
Or else we circle the same centers.

Drove to Ledges State Park, that canyon,
and was afraid of the man who noticed
that I was alone, so I turned and moved straight
up the hill and another man, practicing his breath.
I startled him. And then no acknowledgment.
Small inside my body. In Boone, the deli. I called you.

Iowa State Fair, Des Moines. I raced a tornado watch home.
Four miles from Sac the rain started. Green. Hard.
Home. From north-facing windows,
flooding in the street. That two contradictory
impressions could be equally true.

Mineral Point, Wisconsin. August.
A canopy, some kegs. Plein air painters.
Low bridge and a willow tree. We went out
for a margarita. She told me how she still holds
a guilt for asking my brother, a toddler then, to stop
banging on the piano, but I told her I'm pretty sure
he still bangs on the piano and anyway
I doubt he's holding that moment now.

In May, I pulled what flowers hadn't closed from
the bunch and folded them between waxed
brown paper.

I am still inclined to address you in my second
person, though I know this is a gone intimacy.

Not that months point to anything
other than a method of counting back.

And The City

Will the memory abduct the terms
of a shift. For whose benefit
the image of a window, afternoon glare,
slush in the road. Step nearer.
Not too close. The scene shifts before I shift:
a sudden consonance, or the continual problem
of enclosure and becoming.
I recognize myself speaking
and my observation becomes a question.
My sentences have subjectivities and I impose
some order, invoke some image. To hold you.
The weather variable in precisely this way:
thin light, thin sleep,
and clear blue into gray.
What exactly are the physics of this shift.

Vignette

Designating the season imposes a timeline. For reproducing
weathering, or weather. Vision in the deep freeze.
How things thread together: a domestic scene, wide open.
Last night the room was scenic. Then in the hour between
sleep and waking, an invented snow. *A countable
bit of rain,* she wrote from California. I held a narrative
throughline, or an image next to a question.

Then three types of taking as consequences of silence.
Cold, a dry flurry. Kettle spitting on the hotplate.
I hadn't even read the text in full—only drawn
conclusions from paragraphs, particular paragraphs. Sun,
ice, juice. A swimmy feeling in my head.
That a scene has transpired, but an uneasy sense of surety.
Ob-scene, in the sense that something's bent.

Late Summer

The heat makes the fields smell like rot.
I wonder if I will remember this—

Gravel trucks every morning, three minutes apart
It was a nice little house til all the birds moved in
Farming velvet off the antlers

After the fair, firefly hour.
I follow the deer and the bats beside
the bean field on my bike—

Vignette

Just beyond countyline, blue chicory.
I stopped to pull at stems, held on to this
blue tangle all the way to Omaha, where
all but one bloom had closed.

Only a string of unrelated coincidences
or a desire for the feeling of momentum (of
healing) (a stop sign of the mind)

We go forward or we go back
or time collapses on the orchard, a process
like this reasonably well understood, though
not sufficient for change. We could not
palate this shortsightedness. (Wished to.)

Vignette

Bean field north of town. Against the clarity
of the day the storm has darkness without
any depth, like a bruise, or like the sorrow
of the river that cleaves the town, dense
and chemical. Astonishing the disquiet
we sustain, as if a motive might become
pure. As if the reading would sate the desire,
and if one speaks of the dream in such terms
it may signal an overwhelm or a dislodge
or never a subjectivity—all conjured
in the moment by the tone not to define
the subjectivity but to denote how embodied
the perceiving—

I have a dream of a new exemption in my
language: singular and continuous *except*
that it can be spoken and what can't
repeats on its own terms—

Even if closeness does not comfort.
Even if closeness is dim and vague and large
I am in some small way awake, and I wait—

Late Summer

Query:
Where will it go?

I have missed you, imperceptible as some progress is,

this slow wasting.

By the nature of parameterization, only one or two opportunities
for a stable compound.

And the whole false lake burned.

April

In the mirror I could not meet my own eye.

How many sides does a stop sign have. Count them.

August Vignette

I overturn potatoes.

I am handed a tangle of beets.

Pick only the brightest red. Cut grass,

corn tasseling. Meat still frozen.

He tips tabasco into his beer.

Green evening, church-bell lullaby.

Insistence of the acorns—

        acorns is not a beautiful word.

July

Bicycled to the county fair. Same thin jokes
in and out. A baseball cap eyeing me by
the tractor pull. Grease on my thighs
when I slide behind the frame.

On the telephone, the small relief
of your voice. I had said again
the thing about gut feelings
and entering a room.

That you forgave it. Or that
the novel ends mid-sentence.

Early Street

The new water treatment building and the
abandoned one. Pit of white gravel.
No land anywhere is unaccounted for. "There is never
anyone down here," I say, and then a deer.
Absent to you. We were alone in our
heads and watching the five unfolding.
An even watching, and just. Incidental to.

I was obscure and remote.
Baked a gift pie to pull myself out,
buttermilk and cinnamon, but the melted
butter rose to the surface and did not turn
properly golden—

Autumn

Understories

Autumn, nearly winter,
very nearly bare:
the overwhelming indifference
of the forest, and the animate
slowness of it.

I felt, at this point,
the development of two
distinct but simultaneous
awarenesses,
and I feel heavy at the thought
that I am absent from
that clearing.

There have been times when limbs or entire trees have fallen on private structures. This is considered an act of God and damage from the falling tree is covered under the individual's insurance.

Vignette

It is helpful to inhabit the moment without any fixation.
Your voice is soft but full of authority.
Cold synesthesia as incurable.

Blue dusk on snow.
I can say easily that I know you, but I have the wrong set
of points of social reference for conversation here.

The stand of trees marks a concealed river. An apple orchard
north of town. I ignored the violet mist.

No Cadence

Storm Lake, Tyson plant, a college.
Without a static boundary

between I do and have done.
Or what I do not believe to be true.

I drove for groceries. The Walmart, the Hy-Vee.
What is still reactive: that defenses failed

to deflect. That a Minnesota
June intrudes. Brief chiaroscuro

of morning. Or a gone July, but
fireworks. Last night I walked

the woods by the river
for the first time since autumn,

and the path was not as I had been thinking
of it. A shudder, sudden fear.

All Along Here

Coercions. Damp morning,
early sun on August-

high cornfields. March.
Kansas City, labyrinth. Day,

day. Or was it April,
subsequent April. Stand

of trees budding,
bending under new

weather. Or:
a kind of surety.

What kind.

September

What is this quality of duration, this resolution

or the way resolve turns itself over

stone fruit, strong coffee, sorting sense from sense

turning the oven on and off, running the laundry, opening

and closing windows

tending the garden (winged things)

a repetition of something basically present

or maybe irreducible

and then, by turns, some other joy, or the dream of a citrus tree

I would like, sometimes, to suspend

my suspicion and inhabit—

inhabit is a domestic word—

a sense of holding the instant close, or to allow

a certain structure to emerge,

an awareness of a narrativity

a narrative perspective, experience the staged-ness of things

a gaze or a smile or a displacement and cultivate new meaning

nights and sleeves and impressions, name them in

a sort of soundscape

a description, some principles of structure

or to suspend what I perceive as difficult

this slow wasting

Over-Spring

She died seated upright, he said, easy chair, half a cupcake
on a circular plate and a fork in her other hand. He said,
"Until then, I had believed death always meant violence."

I had this impression that the town was full of people
who had ended up here by accident. I would go away for a day
or two and return, always by Highway 20, westbound.

Coda

How Many Encounters

Through what process of division should my attention fall

on this heat   over milk

                                                  turning over velvet

The man in the next room has a cough in his ribcage

Insufficient that you should simply experience

this exchange as time

Unable or unwilling to consider me head-on and also

from the head down

Against what I have interrogated and diminished

I want only the scaffold and not its application

Or how else will this movement modify my limbs

But the pressure and waste of you in your gesture

And the city very brightly laid in brick

My heels clip on the inlaid brick

A private insistence like some immovable lake

with a relationship to that summer,

if a negative one   one of absence

Or something of cardamom

You are present and become altered

When it began to storm I leaned out of my window and so

did a man across the courtyard

to flip the switch on a round fan facing inside

                    109 degrees, you remember

The light in my room was not on but he looked to me

Paused

I backed into the shadow behind the left window

We lingered

He turned off the fan turned out his light

Always the impulse to favor one perspective

over another

❖ Notes ❖

Sources include the Lake View community newsletter, various studies on the Raccoon River in Sac County, and media coverage of the 2015 Des Moines Water Works lawsuit. Italicization references these, a linguistics textbook I've misplaced, or otherwise things people said to me in Iowa.

Other works and languages tended to in this writing:

Sandy Berrigan, *Daily Rites*

Elizabeth Bishop & Robert Lowell, *Words in Air: The Complete Correspondence*

Dionne Brand, *The Blue Clerk: Ars Poetica in 59 Versos*

H.D., *Notes on Thought and Vision*

Tom Drury, *The End of Vandalism*

Barbara Guest, *Seeking Air*, *Collected Poems*, and *Forces of Imagination*

Myung Mi Kim, *Commons*

Robin Wall Kimmerer, *Braiding Sweetgrass: Indigenous Wisdom, Scientific Knowledge and the Teachings of Plants*

Marie Mutsuki Mockett, *American Harvest: God, Country, and Farming in the Heartland*

Rob Nixon, *Slow Violence and the Environmentalism of the Poor*

Lisa Robertson, *Cinema of the Present*

Kathryn Scanlan, *Aug 9—Fog*

R. Murray Schafer, *The Soundscape: Our Sonic Environment and the Tuning of the World*

John Stilgoe, *What Is Landscape?*

Anna Lowenhaupt Tsing, *The Mushroom at the End of the World*

Sarah Vap, *Winter: Effulgences, Devotions*

Thornton Wilder, *The Eighth Day*

❖ Thank You ❖

Thank you Alex Toy, Leah Nieboer, Stella Corso, Liana Jahan Imam, and Zack Rybak for thinking with me. Thank you Graham Foust, Lindsay Turner, and Prageeta Sharma for time and guidance, and thank you Joanna Howard for sentient ecologies. Thank you Sandra Lim, Katie Peterson, Hadley Hendrix, and Megan Gravendyk Estrella. Thank you Tony Legato for lettering *Surety* and for being my home. This book began before her but is published in the era of Bertie.

❖ About the Author ❖

ANNA ZUMBAHLEN holds a PhD in English & Literary Arts from the University of Denver and lives in Southern California.

✣ About Inlandia Institute ✣

The Inlandia Institute is an Inland Southern California-based literary and cultural arts non-profit and publishing house. We seek to bring focus to the richness of the literary enterprise that has existed in this region for ages.

The mission of Inlandia Books is to recognize, support, and expand literary activity in Inland Southern California by publishing works which deepen people's awareness, understanding, and appreciation of this unique, complex and creatively vibrant region. The mission is carried out by actively seeking out new works by writers who are affiliated with the region, and also through national literary competitions which elevate Inlandia Books to the national literary stage.

To learn more about the Inlandia Institute, please visit our website at www.InlandiaInstitute.org.

✥ The Hillary Gravendyk Prize ✥

The Hillary Gravendyk Prize is awarded annually for two full-length collections of poetry: one national and one representing the Inland Southern California region. Each winner receives a monetary prize of $1,000 and book publication through Inlandia Books.

HILLARY GRAVENDYK (1979–2014) was a beloved poet living and teaching in Southern California's "Inland Empire" region. She wrote the acclaimed poetry book *Harm* (Omnidawn, 2012) and the posthumously published *The Soluble Hour (*Omnidawn, 2017) as well as *Unlikely Conditions,* with Cynthia Arrieu-King (1913 Press, 2017) and the poetry chapbook *The Naturalist* (Achiote Press, 2008). A native of Washington State, she was an admired Assistant Professor of English at Pomona College in Claremont, CA. Hillary Gravendyk was two-time winner of the Eisner Prize in Poetry and was awarded a 2015 Pushcart Prize for her poem "Your Ghost," which appeared in the *Pushcart Prize Anthology*. She passed away on May 10, 2014 after a long illness. This contest was established in her memory.

❖ The Hillary Gravendyk Prize Poetry Series ❖

Condition by Meg Reynolds
Winner of the 2024 National Hillary Gravendyk Prize

Surety by Anna Zumbahlen
Winner of the 2024 Regional Hillary Gravendyk Prize

pain survey by Jennifer Mackenzie
Winner of the 2023 National Hillary Gravendyk Prize

Law of the Letter by Elizabeth Galoozis
Winner of the 2023 Regional Hillary Gravendyk Prize

the artemisia by William S. Barnes
Winner of the 2022 National Hillary Gravendyk Prize

Bones Awaiting the Blaze by Tiffany Elliott
Winner of the 2022 Regional Hillary Gravendyk Prize

How to Know You're Dreaming When You're Dreaming
by Angelica Maria Barraza Tran
Winner of the 2021 National Hillary Gravendyk Prize

Our Lady of Perpetual Desert by Alexandra Martinez
Winner of the 2021 Regional Hillary Gravendyk Prize

among the enemies by Michael Samra
Winner of the 2020 National Hillary Gravendyk Prize

This Side of the Fire by Jonathan Maule
Winner of the 2020 Regional Hillary Gravendyk Prize

The Silk the Moths Ignore by Bronwen Tate
Winner of the 2019 National Hillary Gravendyk Prize

Remyth: A Postmodernist Ritual by Adam Martinez
Winner of the 2019 Regional Hillary Gravendyk Prize

Former Possessions of the Spanish Empire
by Michelle Peñaloza
Winner of the 2018 National Hillary Gravendyk Prize

All the Emergency-Type Structures by Elizabeth Cantwell
Winner of the 2018 Regional Hillary Gravendyk Prize

Our Bruises Kept Singing Purple by Malcolm Friend
Winner of the 2017 National Hillary Gravendyk Prize

Traces of a Fifth Column by Marco Maisto
Winner of the 2016 National Hillary Gravendyk Prize

God's Will for Monsters by Rachelle Cruz
Winner of the 2016 Regional Hillary Gravendyk Prize
Winner of the 2018 American Book Award

Map of an Onion by Kenji C. Liu
Winner of the 2015 National Hillary Gravendyk Prize

All Things Lose Thousands of Times by Angela Peñaredondo
Winner of the 2015 Regional Hillary Gravendyk Prize

www.ingramcontent.com/pod-product-compliance
Lightning Source LLC
LaVergne TN
LVHW091010080826
845145LV00003B/1216

* 9 7 8 1 9 5 5 9 6 9 5 4 3 *